Big Machines

Big Machines Ride Rails!

Catherine Veitch

Heinemann
LIBRARY
Chicago, Illinois

Contents

Big Boy Locomotive 4

Bullet Train. 6

Railroad Snowplow 8

Hanging Train. 10

Eurostar 12

Bilevel Rail Car 14

Monorail 16

Roller Ride. 18

Sizing Things Up 20

Quiz 22

Glossary. 23

Find Out More 24

Index 24

Some words are shown in bold, **like this.** You can find out what they mean by looking in the glossary.

Big Boy Locomotive

Big Boy was a huge train, or **locomotive**. It could pull up to 120 **freight cars** at once.

Big Boy 4012 is now on display at a railroad museum.

Super
Big Mighty
Size

Big Boy weighs just under 600 tons (544 metric tons).

Bullet Train

Bullet trains are fast **passenger** trains. Their **streamlined** shape helps them travel quickly.

Tunnels have been built for trains to travel straight through mountains!

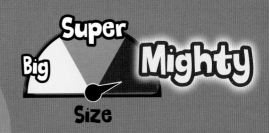

Big **Super** **Mighty**
Size

The Taiwan High Speed Rail reaches speeds of 186 miles (300 kilometers) per hour.

Railroad Snowplow

Railroad snowplows can be as tall as houses. The driver climbs a ladder attached to the side of the machine to get in.

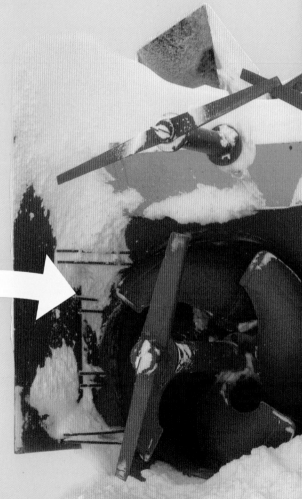

Huge metal blades push snow off the tracks.

Hanging Train

This train is not upside down. It's hanging from a track!

Hanging trains were first built in Germany more than 100 years ago. There was no room for a railway track on the ground.

Eurostar

Eurostars travel under the sea between England and France. Builders started building the tunnel from each end. Amazingly, they met in the middle!

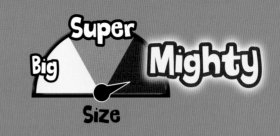

Eurostars reach
speeds of 186 miles
(300 kilometers)
per hour.

Bilevel Rail Car

Bilevel rail cars are trains that have two levels. Passengers can eat, sleep, and shower on these trains.

Bilevel rail cars are also called double-decker coaches.

Monorail

A train that has one track is called a **monorail**. Many big cities have monorails above the ground.

China has the longest monorail track in the world. It is 104 miles (167 kilometers) long.

Roller Ride

Kingda Ka in New Jersey is the tallest roller coaster in the world.

Kingda Ka zooms around a track at speeds up to 128 miles (206 kilometers) per hour.

Sizing Things Up

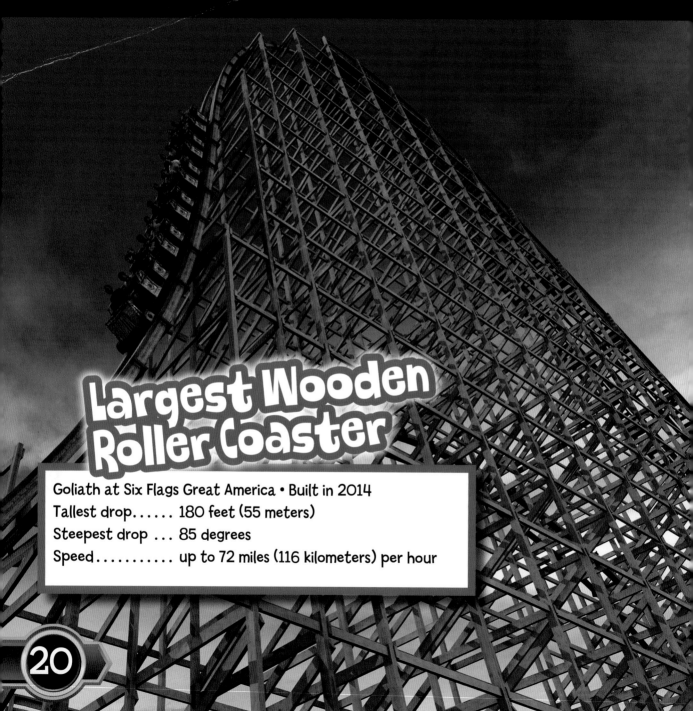

Largest Wooden Roller Coaster

Goliath at Six Flags Great America • Built in 2014

Tallest drop...... 180 feet (55 meters)

Steepest drop ... 85 degrees

Speed........... up to 72 miles (116 kilometers) per hour

Largest Steel Roller Coaster

Kingda Ka at Six Flags Great Adventure • Built in 2005

Tallest drop...... 418 feet (127 meters)
Steepest drop ... 90 degrees
Speed........... up to 128 miles (206 kilometers) per hour

Quiz

How much of a Machine Mega-Brain are you?
Can you match each machine name to its correct photo?

Big Boy • hanging train
bullet train • monorail

1

2

3

4

Check the answers on the opposite page
to see if you got all four correct.

Glossary

freight car the part of a train that carries goods or cargo

locomotive the railroad car that holds the engine to pull the train

monorail a railroad that runs on one rail, usually high above the ground

passenger a person who rides on an airplane, train, or other vehicle

streamlined designed to move easily and quickly through air or water

Find Out More

Books

Bridges, Sarah. *I Drive a Freight Train*. Working Wheels.
    Minneapolis: Picture Window Books, 2006.

Shields, Amy. *Trains*. National Geographic Readers.
    Washington, D.C.: National Geographic, 2011.

Websites

www.bbc.co.uk/learningzone/clips/trains-are-fantastic/11185.html
www.easyscienceforkids.com/all-about-trains/

Index

B
Big Boy 4, 5
bilevel rail cars 14
bullet trains 6, 7
E
Eurostars 12, 13
F
freight cars 4
G
Goliath 20

H
hanging trains 10
K
Kingda Ka 18, 19, 21
L
locomotives 4
M
monorails 16, 17
P
passenger trains 6, 14

R
railroad snowplows 8
roller coasters 18, 19, 20, 21
T
Taiwan High Speed Rail 7